National Parks
Bryce Canyon

JENNIFER HACKETT

Children's Press®
An Imprint of Scholastic Inc.

Content Consultant
James Gramann, PhD
Professor Emeritus, Department of Recreation, Park and Tourism Sciences
Texas A&M University, College Station, Texas

Library of Congress Cataloging-in-Publication Data
Names: Hackett, Jennifer, author.
Title: Bryce Canyon / by Jennifer Hackett.
Description: New York, NY : Children's Press, an imprint of Scholastic Inc., 2019. | Series: A true
    book | Includes bibliographical references and index.
Identifiers: LCCN 2018032564| ISBN 9780531129319 (library binding) | ISBN 9780531135006 (pbk.)
Subjects: LCSH: Bryce Canyon National Park (Utah)—Juvenile literature. | National parks and
    reserves—United States—Juvenile literature.
Classification: LCC F832.B9 H325 2019 | DDC 979.2/52—dc23
LC record available at https://lccn.loc.gov/2018032564

Scholastic Inc., 557 Broadway, New York, NY 10012

1 2 3 4 5 6 7 8 9 10 R 28 27 26 25 24 23 22 21 20 19

**Front cover (main): A hiker among
hoodoos in the Queen's Garden**
Front cover (inset): A skier
Back cover: Visitors on a horse trail

Find the Truth!

Everything you are about to read is true *except* for one of the sentences on this page.

Which one is **TRUE**?

T or F A hoodoo is an oddly shaped pillar of rock formed by erosion.

T or F Most of Bryce Canyon's rain falls in its lowest areas.

Find the answers in this book.

Contents

THE **BIG** TRUTH!

National Parks Field Guide: Bryce Canyon

Peregrine falcon

Trees and shrubs

Mountain lion

Bryce Canyon is not really a canyon. But its amphitheaters looked like a canyon to the people who named it.

The Beginning of Bryce

★Bryce Canyon National Park

Looking out into an **amphitheater** at Bryce Canyon is amazing. Located high on the Colorado Plateau, the rippling red rock towers and limestone cliffs look like an artist carved them. Trails take visitors past evergreen trees and waterfalls. When the sky is clear, you can see land miles away during the day and thousands of stars at night. Visiting Bryce Canyon is like visiting another world!

The First People

People roamed the area around Bryce Canyon as early as 12,000 years ago. The Numa, sometimes called the Paiute, first arrived in about 1200 CE. Some live in the region today. The park's wavy rock pillars, called hoodoos, are part of the Numa mythology. The Numa believe the pillars are spirits that overused the land's resources. As punishment, Coyote, a trickster god, turned the spirits into rock.

A Timeline of Bryce Canyon National Park

10,000 BCE

Native Americans start living in the area.

1850s

Mormon scouts explore the area looking for possible settlement locations.

1872

A scientific expedition explores the region as part of a survey of the Colorado Plateau.

Science and Settlements

The first European Americans reached Bryce Canyon in the 19th century. Some of these explorers were scientists **surveying** the region. Others were Mormon scouts looking for a place to build a settlement. The park earned its current name during this time. Ebenezer Bryce, a Mormon settler, built a road into the park's main amphitheater. Because of this road, the amphitheater was called Bryce Canyon.

1916
Magazine articles from railroad companies and the U.S. Forest Service describe the area's natural beauty.

1923
President Warren G. Harding declares Bryce Canyon a national monument.

1928
Bryce Canyon becomes a national park.

Today
Bryce Canyon National Park is one of Utah's most popular parks.

Bryce Canyon National Park became one of southern Utah's "Mighty 5" national parks.

Protection and Popularity

In the early 1900s, Bryce Canyon was still not well known and was difficult to reach. Then in 1916, U.S. Forest Service worker J. W. Humphrey brought in photographers and helped write articles about Bryce Canyon. He also built roads to make traveling in the area easier.

Bryce Canyon gained fame, and Utah lawmakers recommended that it be protected. In 1923, President Warren G. Harding declared Bryce Canyon a national monument. The U.S. Congress then passed a law that made it a national park in 1928.

National Park Fact File

A national park is land that is protected by the federal government. It is a place of importance to the United States because of its beauty, history, or value to scientists. The U.S. Congress creates a national park by passing a law. Here are some key facts about Bryce Canyon National Park.

Bryce Canyon National Park	
Location	Southwestern Utah
Year established	1928
Size	56 square miles (145 square kilometers)
Average number of visitors each year	About 1.5 million
Number of stars seen at night	7,500
Highest point in the park	Rainbow Point, at 9,105 feet (2,775 meters)
Famous features	Hoodoos, cliffs, evergreen forests

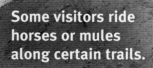

Some visitors ride horses or mules along certain trails.

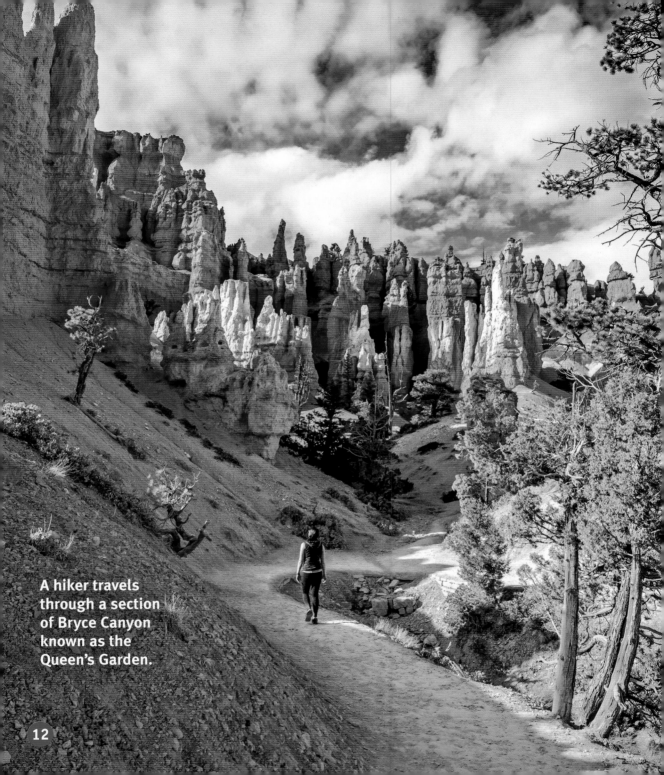

A hiker travels through a section of Bryce Canyon known as the Queen's Garden.

CHAPTER 2

Amazing Amphitheaters

It took millions of years for Bryce Canyon to become the strange and beautiful place it is today. Layers of different colored rocks built up over time. Water, ice, and wind slowly carved the park's hoodoos and cliffs out of these layers. The rocks that make up Bryce Canyon's hoodoos are 30 million to 40 million years old!

 More than 50 miles (80 km) of trails wind through the park.

A Misleading Name

Bryce Canyon isn't actually a canyon. A canyon is formed by a river wearing away a path over hundreds of years. Instead, the land was shaped mainly through a type of erosion called frost wedging. Water flowed into cracks in the rock. When the water froze at night, it expanded and chipped away at the rock. Over time, erosion expanded these cracks into large open areas called amphitheaters.

The hoodoo called Thor's Hammer is so named because its shape looks like that mythical object.

Land starts as a single, whole section of rock.

Over time, erosion reshapes the land. Cracks appear.

Snow and ice freeze in the cracks, and the cracks expand.

The cracks become large openings, leaving separate rock pillars.

What's a Hoodoo?

Frost wedging also formed Bryce Canyon's spectacular rock pillars, called hoodoos. Rainwater wore away at the pillars, too, creating their unusual shapes. Today, Bryce Canyon has more hoodoos than anyplace in the world! But erosion doesn't stop. Over time, the hoodoos that now stand in the park will be worn completely away, leaving only colorful mounds behind.

Skiing through Bryce Canyon can be just as exciting as a summertime hike.

Hiking and Skiing

Miles of park trails showcase Bryce Canyon's beauty. One of the most popular is the Rim Trail. It takes visitors past many famous sights, such as Sunrise and Sunset Points. Most trails wind past hoodoos such as Thor's Hammer or wander deep into the park to Mossy Cave and its waterfall. During the winter, some people even cross-country ski or snowshoe around the park. The snow causes the hoodoos to look even brighter in color.

Loop Through New and Old

In Bryce, you can see firsthand how time changes the landscape. Take a hike along the Fairyland Loop Trail. The first major site you'll see are the hoodoos at Fairyland Canyon. These rock formations are among the park's youngest. They are tall and rough. Continue on the trail to Campbell Canyon and you'll see something very different. It's a hoodoo graveyard. The hoodoos here have already eroded over millions of years to just multicolored mounds!

Hoodoo graveyard

Young Steps

Bryce Canyon contains part of the Grand Staircase. The Grand Staircase is a huge set of **sedimentary** rock layers. It stretches across Bryce Canyon, Zion, and Grand Canyon national parks. Each layer is a different color, including pink, white, and red. The oldest layers are on the bottom, and the youngest are at the top. In Bryce Canyon, visitors can see the youngest layers, which are about 40 million years old. Older layers are underground.

Streaks of colors run through each step in the Grand Staircase.

Each June, hundreds of stargazers visit the park for its annual Astronomy Festival.

Clear Skies

The sky over Bryce Canyon is amazingly clear. The park's distance from cities means it doesn't experience light pollution and smog. During the day, you can spot mountains and peaks up to 150 miles (241 km) away. At night, the sky is exceptionally dark. That makes it perfect for stargazing!

The yellow-rumped warbler can be spotted in the park in summer.

CHAPTER 3

Life in the Sky and Underground

From the forested plateau to the dry amphitheaters, there are many places in the park for animals to make home. The population of animals in the park is always changing as animals come and go. Many animals are **migratory**. They stop in the park to find water and shade, but move on. You might find different animals in Bryce Canyon depending on what time of year you visit!

More than twice as many bird species can be seen in Bryce Canyon in summer than in winter.

California condors had nearly gone extinct when scientists began breeding them to help increase their numbers.

Taking Flight

Only a few bird species live in the park year-round. In spring and summer, ospreys fish in the park's Tropic Reservoir and peregrine falcons soar overhead. The most exciting bird to spot is the **endangered** California condor. If you see this rare bird, be sure to tell a ranger! Scientists use this information in their work to save the birds.

Under Your Feet

Spotting animals on the ground is also a popular pastime in the park. There are 59 mammals that live in Bryce Canyon's various regions. Golden squirrels and Uinta chipmunks scurry through all parts of the park. Pronghorn antelope live in flat, bushy areas. Mountain lions prowl the park's roads at night, leaving behind tracks that visitors can spot during the day.

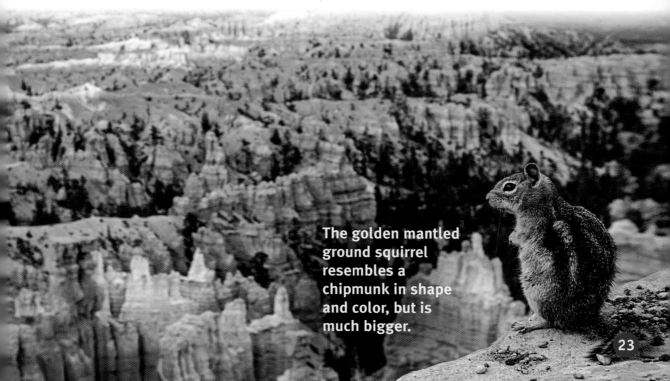

The golden mantled ground squirrel resembles a chipmunk in shape and color, but is much bigger.

Slithering and Sunning

Only 11 reptiles and four amphibians live in Bryce Canyon National Park. The park's high altitude and cold nights make it difficult for these cold-blooded animals. The bodies of warm-blooded animals, such as humans, produce their own heat. Cold-blooded animals do not. They need warmth from their environment to function.

Short-horned lizards are found throughout the park. With their gray and red- or yellow-brown coloring, they blend in with the rocky environment. The only venomous reptile here is the Great Basin rattlesnake.

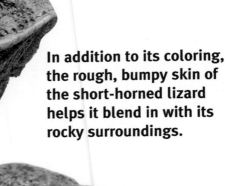

In addition to its coloring, the rough, bumpy skin of the short-horned lizard helps it blend in with its rocky surroundings.

Utah Prairie Dog

The Utah prairie dog is a threatened species that is **endemic** to southwestern Utah. It is only found there. The biggest population of these mammals—nearly 200 prairie dogs—makes Bryce Canyon home. The tawny brown creatures live in burrows underground. Their burrows help them hide from predators, such as coyotes. These critters are an important part of Bryce Canyon's ecosystem.

National Parks Field Guide:
Bryce Canyon

Here are a few of the hundreds of fascinating animals you may see in the park.

Great Basin rattlesnake

Scientific name: *Crotalus viridis lutosus*

Habitat: Rocky areas, slopes, canyons

Diet: Small mammals, reptiles, amphibians, birds

Fact: This snake is venomous. Its venom, or poison, enters its prey through the snake's hollow fangs.

North American porcupine

Scientific name: *Erethizon dorsatum*

Habitat: Forests, grasslands, rocky areas

Diet: Plant parts, including berries, seeds, leaves, roots, and stems

Fact: One porcupine has about 30,000 spines, called quills.

Pronghorn antelope

Scientific name: *Antilocapra americana*

Habitat: Meadows and other open areas

Diet: Shrubs such as sagebrush

Fact: Pronghorns are the second-fastest land animal on earth. Only cheetahs are faster.

Peregrine falcon

Scientific name: *Falco peregrinus anatum*

Habitat: Forests, high rocky areas

Diet: Birds such as ducks and pigeons

Fact: Male peregrines use their expert flying skills to attract mates.

Southwestern willow flycatcher

Scientific name: *Empidonax traillii extimus*

Habitat: Near rivers and streams

Diet: Flying and crawling insects

Fact: This endangered species darts from its perch to catch flying insects in midair.

Mule deer

Scientific name: *Odocoileus hemionus*

Habitat: Forests and open, rocky areas

Diet: Grasses, leaves, flowers, fruits

Fact: When mule deer run, they leap, landing on and pushing off with all four feet at once.

28

CHAPTER 4

Forest Zones

Bryce Canyon is a pocket of green above its **arid** surroundings. More than 400 species of plants add color and life to the park. Animals and insects rely on the plants for food and shelter. There are many types of trees, shrubs, and wildflowers throughout the park's different regions.

It takes 100 years to wear away 2 to 4 feet (0.6 to 1.2 m) of rock!

Blue flax provides food to deer, antelope, and many birds.

At the Bottom

The lower parts of the park are rich with pinyon pine and juniper forests. Gambel oaks, cactuses, and yuccas also dot the landscape. Wildflowers like the poisonous mountain death-camas, the bush cinquefoil, and the blue flax add color to trails. Bryce Canyon's lower **elevations** receive less rain than those higher up. These plants can survive in the dry climate.

In the Middle

The middle elevations of Bryce Canyon are home to forests of ponderosa pines. These large trees were once used for lumber. The trees thrive in drier areas. You might notice something sweet in the air when surrounded by these trees. The bark smells like vanilla or butterscotch! Manzanita shrubs fill the rest of the landscape.

The setting sun shines over a field of manzanita shrubs.

This tree in Bryce Canyon uses its roots to cling to the rocky cliff.

At the Top

The oldest trees in the park are in the higher elevations. Some, such as the bristlecone pine, can live for thousands of years. The oldest one in Bryce Canyon is found on the Bristlecone Loop Trail. Aspens, as well as evergreens such as Engelmann spruces and white firs, fill in the landscape. Wildflowers like the rare Bryce Canyon paintbrush are also found here. The Bryce Canyon paintbrush is endemic. It only grows in this region.

Bryce Canyon's Plants

High Elevations

Evergreens, many of them ancient, thrive here. So do wildflowers and other low-growing plants.

Bristlecone pine tree

Bryce Canyon paintbrush

Middle Elevations

Pine forests and scrubland are found in the middle elevations.

Ponderosa pine tree

Manzanita shrub

Low Elevations

Hardy trees, both evergreen and deciduous (losing their leaves each fall), and other plants grow here.

Mountain death-camas

Pinyon pine

A crew member cuts apart a tree as part of a process called forest thinning, which helps limit the damage that wildfires cause.

CHAPTER 5

Caring for the Canyon

National parks are established to protect some of the country's most beautiful places. It's the job of park rangers to preserve the plants, animals, and geological features that make up the parks. As visitors pass through the park and human activities impact it, this job becomes more challenging. Park rangers, scientists, and the public have to work together to keep the park safe.

Despite the yellow color of its flowers, dyer's woad leaves can be used to make a blue dye.

Unwelcome Guests

Invasive plants such as dyer's woad and yellow star thistle could hurt Bryce Canyon's native ecosystem. These plants are not native to the area. They grow quickly and prevent native plants from getting the water and resources they need to thrive. Park rangers have many tools to control invasive species. They use fire and chemicals, and sometimes clear plants by hand.

The Role of a Ranger

Park rangers help visitors get the most out of a trip to Bryce Canyon. Some rangers are experts in the park's plants, animals, and natural wonders. Others are the park's protectors. They make sure visitors stay safe, follow the rules, and don't damage delicate plant and animal life or rock formations. Many rangers also conduct scientific studies about how the weather and other factors are changing the park. No one knows Bryce Canyon better than its rangers!

A park ranger in Bryce Canyon National Park

Cars driving near or through the park produce both air pollution and light pollution.

Pushing Back on Pollution

Bryce Canyon's clear air is one of its most impressive features. Rangers are particularly concerned with the park's **visibility**. Dust and pollution in the park's air from visitors' cars, as well as power plants and outside traffic, can cause haze. This limits how far guests can see.

Light pollution is also a concern for the park's nighttime views. Artificial light sources as far as 200 miles (322 km) away from the park can make it harder to see the night sky.

Acid rain is another issue. Acid rain is rainwater that is made harmful by air pollution from fossil fuels such as gasoline or coal. It erodes rocks faster than cleaner water or wind. Bryce Canyon's rock formations are particularly at risk because of this.

Rangers monitor the amount of pollution in the air. They also educate visitors about how to care for the park and other natural areas. With everyone's help, Bryce Canyon will be enjoyed for many years to come. ★

Bryce Canyon's unique beauty makes it an important place to protect.

Map Mystery

Bryce Canyon is home to countless natural wonders. Follow the clues below to find an overlook that offers a view of many of these beauties, including Thor's Hammer.

Directions

1. Start at the Visitor Center. Hop on a shuttle bus headed south along the park road all the way to Rainbow Point. You'll want to save your energy for the hike back!

2. Hike north until you reach a point named after a land of magical creatures.

3. Head southeast to a rock that is shaped like a ship that is sinking.

4. Travel southwest to a point named for the sunrise. Almost there!

5. Go south until you reach an overlook named for the opposite time of day. It's the perfect place to watch the sun go down!

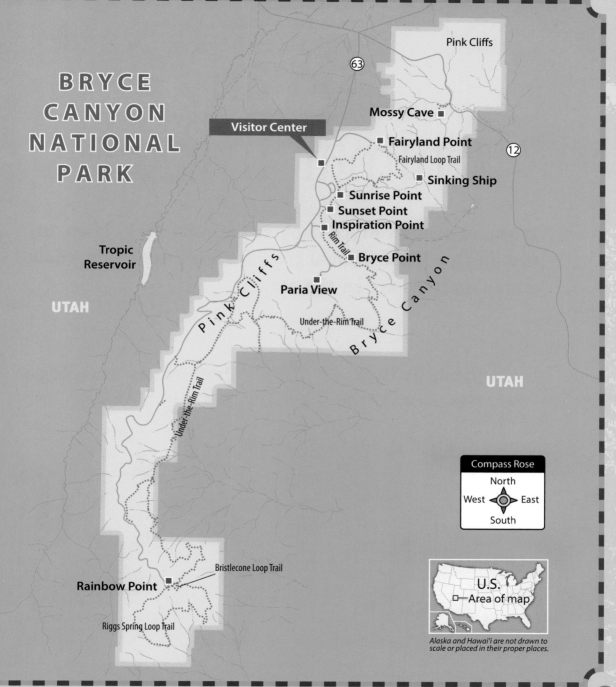

BRYCE CANYON NATIONAL PARK

Pink Cliffs

63

Visitor Center

Mossy Cave

Fairyland Point

Fairyland Loop Trail

12

Sinking Ship

Sunrise Point

Sunset Point

Inspiration Point

Rim Trail

Tropic Reservoir

Bryce Point

Pink Cliffs

UTAH

Paria View

Bryce Canyon

Under-the-Rim Trail

UTAH

Under-the-Rim Trail

Compass Rose

North

West ◆ East

South

Bristlecone Loop Trail

Rainbow Point

U.S.

□ Area of map

Riggs Spring Loop Trail

Alaska and Hawai'i are not drawn to scale or placed in their proper places.

Be an Animal Tracker!

If you're ever in Bryce Canyon National Park, keep an eye out for these animal tracks. They'll help you know which animals are in the area.

Mountain lion
Paw length: 3 inches (7.6 cm)

Pronghorn antelope
Hoof length: 3.25 inches (8.3 cm)

Utah prairie dog
Paw length: 1.5 inches (3.8 cm)

Tiger salamander
Foot length: 0.7 inches (1.8 cm)

Wild turkey
Foot length: 4.5 inches (11.4 cm)

Coyote
Paw length: 2.5 inches (6.4 cm)

True Statistics

Distance of farthest mountains a person can see while standing in Bryce Canyon National Park: 150 mi. (241 km)

Height of tallest hoodoo in the park: 150 ft. (46 m)

Length of the park's scenic drive: 18 mi. (29 km)

Number of bird species found in the park: 175

Number of mammal species that live in the park: 59

Number of reptile and amphibian species: 15

Number of insect species: More than 1,000

Number of plant species: More than 400

Did you find the truth?

T A hoodoo is an oddly shaped pillar of rock formed by erosion.

F Most of Bryce Canyon's rain falls in its lowest areas.

Resources

Books

Gregory, Josh. *Utah*. New York: Children's Press, 2018.

McHugh, Erin. *National Parks: A Kid's Guide to America's Parks, Monuments, and Landmarks*. New York: Black Dog & Leventhal, 2012.

Visit this Scholastic website for more information on Bryce Canyon National Park:

★ www.factsfornow.scholastic.com
Enter the keywords **Bryce Canyon**

Important Words

acid rain (AS-id RAYN) rain that is polluted by chemicals in the air, damaging lakes, forests, buildings, and other objects

amphitheater (AM-fih-thee-uh-tur) large, open area of rock surrounded by high cliffs

arid (AR-id) extremely dry because of a lack of rain

elevations (el-uh-VAY-shuhnz) heights above sea level

endangered (en-DAYN-jurd) at risk of becoming extinct, usually because of human activity

endemic (en-DEH-mik) native to a particular place and not native anywhere else

invasive (in-VAY-sihv) of or having to do with entering a place in large numbers, usually with a negative effect

migratory (MYE-gruh-tor-ee) of or relating to the regular movement of animals from one region to another

sedimentary (sed-uh-MEN-tur-ee) of or relating to a type of rock that is formed by layers of rock, sand, or dirt that have been pressed together

surveying (sur-VAY-ing) measuring the lines and angles of a piece of land in order to make a map or plan

visibility (viz-uh-BIHL-uh-tee) the ability to see

Index

Page numbers in **bold** indicate illustrations.

About the Author

Jennifer Hackett studied physics and history at the College of William and Mary. After deciding she wanted to write instead of research, she attended New York University's Science, Health, and Environmental Reporting Program. She currently works as Scholastic MATH's associate editor. She loves stargazing and hiking, so Bryce Canyon sounds like a dream trip!